The Roman ~~~~~~~~~ ~~uced the engagement ring as a sign of possession. However, the wedding ring is a symbol of harmony and unity.

❀ ❀

The Greeks considered that the third finger on the left hand was connected by a vein to the heart; hence, it is the common ring finger.

THE QUINTESSENTIAL WEDDING GUIDE

Best Man

BY HEIDI L. HOLMES

Holmes, Heidi L.
The Quintessential Wedding Guide
Best Man / By Heidi L. Holmes ("Author")
http://www.blueinkdesigns.com

ISBN 978-0-9805263-2-5

Printed and bound by CPI Antony Rowe, Eastbourne

Published by Holmes Futures PL, Australia ("Publisher")
http://www.holmesfutures.com

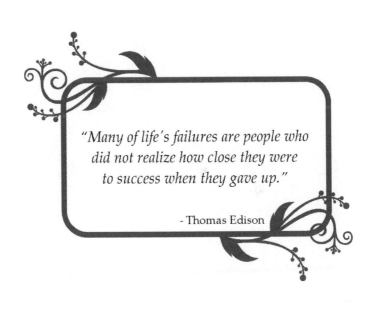

"Many of life's failures are people who did not realize how close they were to success when they gave up."

- Thomas Edison

TABLE OF CONTENTS

Introduction

❀ ❀

Chapter One

Chapter Two

Chapter Three

Chapter Four

Chapter Five

Chapter Six

Chapter Seven

Chapter Eight

Chapter Nine

*"The place to be happy is here,
the time to be happy is now."*

- Robert Ingersoll

Introduction

THE HISTORICAL BEST MAN

Weddings have played an important role throughout history. Dating back to the first recorded days of man's descendants, you can find evidence of weddings. Marriages were encouraged so that clans and tribes could continue on with "fresh blood," new children, and build the population for survival.

Centuries ago, the best man and the maid of honor were representatives for the bride and the groom's families who were fighting or contesting the marriage. Their role was to be a witness for both families and ensure the wedding actually took place. Remember that this was from a time in history when marriages were arranged for property and money and not love.

As the centuries passed and more marriages occurred, they evolved into being based on love and for expanding family rather than for monetary gain. Along with the changes to the weddings themselves, the traditions of the best man also evolved to the point where he now represents the groom as a witness in the marriage instead of an opposing counterpart to witness the marriage.

Sometime during the eighteenth century, the tradition was for a man to wish the new bride good luck, which is one of the historical duties of the best man.

Wishing luck to the bride before any other person ensures years of happiness for the new couple. This tradition has been replaced whereby pastors or ministers now wish the couple good luck before any other person can.

In ancient times, it was often the duty of the best man to arrange for a gun salute as the bride and groom left the wedding ceremony. The gun salutes have long been removed from wedding traditions and have been replaced by the best man driving the couple around in his car, honking the horn so that everyone takes notice of the newlyweds.

When kings and queens were rulers, a groom would go out to the countryside and "capture" a bride along with the help of his knights. The knights were considered his "best men," and from this time forward, the best man would ride with the groom to find a bride worthy of his attention.

BEST MAN IN MODERN TIMES

In our current society, the best man helps the groom prepare for the wedding, settles any last-minute jitters, helps to finalize any last-minute details, and most importantly, the best man helps the groom enjoy his last days of bachelorhood.

The best man is held responsible for helping the groom make his bride happy by creating memories for the two of them as they seal their love. Whenever the groom thinks back to his bachelor days and the days leading up to his wedding day, he will have great memories of his best man and what he helped him accomplish.

Throughout the country, from the rich to the poor, every groom has a best man. The way you handle your role as the best man will determine how successful you are deemed to be.

The way in which you handle the bachelor party is also important. When planning the bachelor party, be sure not to take things to extremes. Keep in mind that your role is to help lighten the load for the groom. If you handle your role well, more than likely, you will remain friends, and then he can be your best man when you get married.

Think of the reasons that you were chosen by the groom to be his best man. Are you funny, sincere, a great planner, his best friend, or the one whom everyone wants to know? Chances are you are all of these and more, all wrapped up into one person. The role of the best man is important, and you should never take your responsibilities lightly since you were chosen especially for this position!

Complete your duties with nobility and class and be a memory-maker for both the bride and groom. You will be remembered as a cornerstone of happiness on their wedding day.

With all of that said, we will go through exactly what you need to know as the best man and how you will fulfill your duties!

As the best man your role is crucial; you are involved in the preparation, the ceremony, and the celebrations that follow. As you go through your duties, remind yourself that you were chosen as the best man for special reasons.

"Measure yourself by your best moments not by your worst."

- Robert Johnson

Chapter One

WHEN THE NEWS HITS

The possibility is that you have no idea you are about to be asked to stand up for the groom as his best man until you are approached and hear "Will you be my best man?" You should be honored and respond with, "Yes and thank you."

From the minute you accept this important request, you will be making your mark on the groom's life.

Accepting this task immediately after being asked is the first sign that you are responsible enough to take charge and do a great job. You should never need time to think about your answer as this honor is something that may never happen again in your lifetime!

Now that you have accepted the role of best man there are a few things that need to be considered specific to the planning. First, determine the date of the wedding. If the wedding is in the same year that you were asked to be best man, you will have many things to accomplish in a short time frame. On the other hand, if the wedding is not planned until sometime the following year then you have more time to plan, which in reality can sometimes make the task seem larger than it is. Regardless of the date, you will need to plan some time off from work, a few days at the very least. If the wedding is on a Saturday, you most likely will need Friday, Saturday, and Sunday, if possible. If you live out of town, you may need a few extra days so you can recoup before going back to work.

In the majority of weddings, Friday is the day for the wedding rehearsal. This is also the day that the hall often gets decorated, flowers are delivered, and any other last minute "things" needed for the ceremony or the reception are taken care of.

If the wedding is scheduled for a Friday, which has become a popular trend, you may need to make yourself available on Thursday, Friday, and Saturday for the groom.

Another consideration to think about is how this will affect those in your personal life. Will your wife and children be going with you to the wedding, or will you be going alone? If you're single, will you be taking a date or spending your time with the single bridesmaids in the party?

If your family is attending the wedding, you also need to consider the arrangements for new clothes and a ride to and from the ceremony and the reception. Another thought should be given to where they will be sitting during the wedding. Also, what they will be doing while you are busy with your role as best man, and how they will get home while you are occupied with cleanup?

If you have a girlfriend, think about how she would feel if you are unable to spend much time with her. Depending on her personality, she may not be comfortable going with you knowing there will be times that she is left sitting at the table by herself while you are off dancing with the bridesmaids!

If this is a situation where she would be uncomfortable, it might be best to attend the wedding alone. If she does come with you, try to secure her a seat with relatives or friends who can occupy her time. This will allow you the opportunity to perform your duties as best man.

How will you remember the big day? As soon as you know the wedding date, write it down on your calendar at work, on the calendar at home, on your computer reminder book, in your day planner, and anywhere else that you look on a regular basis. Keeping the date in front of you will ensure you do not book something else on that same day or the days you need off to serve as best man.

In addition, you need to be sure you mark the date of the bachelor party on your calendars as well. Once the wedding is scheduled, choose a Friday or Saturday night the weekend before the wedding for the bachelor party. Once this date is determined, start planning.

For more information on this, see the section on bachelor parties for great ideas later in this book.

Whether the wedding is in a few months or a year away, the time to start getting into shape is now. If you have an annoying five pounds to lose, this is a good time to take action. Have your hair styled the way you like it and start working on that tan that you love to show off.

Although these are small things, together they will help you look your very best for the bride and groom. Keep in mind that you will be in many of the wedding pictures, videos, and pages of their memories, so you want to look fantastic!

In review, you need to know the wedding date and then write it down everywhere! Pick a date for the bachelor party to coincide with the wedding. Start getting yourself into shape so you will be your best for the big day. As you move closer to the wedding day, additional dates will be added to your calendar.

Some of these include the date for getting measured for your tuxedo, the date for buying gifts for the couple, the date for picking up your tuxedo, the date for getting everything in order for the bachelor party, time needed for decorating the hall, and other special arrangements that the groom may need help with.

Do not forget that you were chosen to be the best man. You will have great responsibility, so be sure that you do not let the happy couple down when it comes to fulfilling your duties or volunteering for anything that may need to be done.

Not only is this a day for the bride, but you will be helping the groom as well to make this an incredible day for him.

BEFORE THE WEDDING QUESTIONS

Some of your duties as the best man mean that you will be responsible for taking care of important details that the groom trusts you with entirely. This means you will have to ask a few questions to ensure your job goes smoothly.

When you have a chance, ask the groom about some of these topics:

* How many ushers will there be?
* How many people will be in the wedding party?
* Do you need to contact out-of-town ushers about their tuxedos, or will the groom handle this?
* Where should you order the boutonnières?
* When do you need to remind the groom about the wedding license?
* Does the groom have a preference as to when the bachelor party should be held?

- ✿ Do you need to gather information regarding the location for the official photographs?
- ✿ Does the groom have a special gift that he would like to give to his bride at any particular time?
- ✿ Where will the food be taken after the reception?
- ✿ When should the gifts be delivered to their home?
- ✿ What colors will be worn?
- ✿ How should the men's hair be done?
- ✿ Will everyone have flowers?

As you read this book, you will understand the importance of formulating all of your questions at once to avoid adding further stress and burden to the groom.

Although there will be other things that come up, the ones mentioned are some that you can ask the groom about when he is free to talk. Some of these items may be handled by the bride.

Before the Wedding Planning
Tuxedos

The men in the wedding party usually wear tuxedos. Be sure to ask if there are special requests, such as children who will be wearing suits or similar tuxedos. When the final decision is made regarding what everyone will wear, you will need to work with the remainder of the ushers to get them prepared as well.

Many times the bride or groom will choose the place where you will rent your tuxedo. However, if you are from out of town, you may need to have your tuxedo measured and rented from another location. In this case, getting the exact style and type is critical.

The best solution is to rent all of them from a chain location so even people from out of town will have the same color, style, fit, and so on. Shoes can be rented or bought through the tailors as well. If the bride or groom allows, all the men can purchase or rent their shoes from a particular store.

Depending on how formal the wedding is, some brides will allow the men to wear their own dress shoes, but be sure to ask the bride or the groom if nothing was specifically said.

You will also be in charge of the fittings and ordering the tuxedos, so be sure that you get the listing of men and boys who will be in the wedding. This will allow you to contact everyone for fittings and alterations. Writing down all of their names and phone numbers will help you save time as the wedding gets closer and fittings are needed. Be sure to order your attire early.

If the wedding will be held in the height of the wedding season, some stores may be too busy to get everything you need in time. Therefore, never wait until the last minute, and remember that holidays and prom seasons are another time of the year when rentals are busy, and tuxedo shops are low on particular sizes and styles.

All of the suits should be picked out and sized at least four months before the wedding. This will help ensure that everyone gets the type of outfit needed. In most cases, tuxedos are rented, but some men in the party may prefer to buy their own, so keep this option open.

When the outfits are being picked out, take a swatch of the women's dresses so the cummerbund can be matched. If you are responsible for making the choice, this will be very important to the bride.

Remember that the more formal the wedding, the more formal the clothing will be for the celebration. If you have a problem with your weight or being tall or short and the bride or groom has picked out a style that is not flattering to you, it is appropriate to mention this. After all, the bride and groom want their wedding party to look great and may have simply overlooked something. If the choice is still one that does not flatter you, do the best you can with the style chosen.

If you are given a choice, remember that a vest hides an overgrown belly. Additionally, a coat without tails is best for the shorter or exceptionally tall man. Be sure that everyone arrives at the rental center at the same time, and be sure to have the tuxedos measured at least three months before the wedding. The final fitting should be two weeks before the wedding; this will allow enough time for any last-minute alterations. Often mistakes are made, and this allows enough time for them to be corrected.

Do not forget that the best man and the groom are usually in different styles than the ushers and children. During the fittings, be sure that everyone is getting the appropriate style.

After the final fitting, try to encourage everyone to refrain from overindulging in the days before the wedding to avoid any last-minute rush orders for fixing tuxedos that no longer fit. Even a few pounds can make a huge difference, so stay trim until after the wedding!

The groom and the best man sometimes wear special cuff links, often purchased just for this occasion or possibly some that have been inherited or have sentimental value.

Earrings for men and other body piercings should be discussed specifically with the bride and groom as they may not allow these in their wedding photographs. Based on what the bride and groom decide, make sure the ushers and other members of the wedding party know the rules and then follow through with the bride and groom's wishes.

While you are discussing what the men are allowed to wear or not wear, also ask the bride and groom about the men's hairstyle. If the wedding is formal, the men should have new haircuts, sideburns trimmed, and faces shaved or beards and mustaches trimmed. If needed, arrangements should be made approximately two weeks before the wedding to ensure all the ushers and the children in the wedding party are photo-ready.

Retailers are known to give special attention and pricing to the groom and possibly the best man. Do not be nervous about asking for a better price for all the ushers as well, especially if they are in the shop with you. The worst thing anyone can say is no.

Ushers from out of town may need a little extra attention. When you go for your fitting, ask your rental retailer for a measurement card that you can send to out-of-town ushers. Once received, these ushers can take their own measurements and mark them down on the card.

When finished, the measurement card is then sent back to you, allowing you to order everything at the same time from the same place. Depending on the chain store that you are working with, they may or may not be able to order the exact same tuxedo from one region to another.

At least one to two weeks before the wedding day, out-of-town ushers will need to make a trip to your town for the final fitting. Also consider that as the wedding day draws near other alterations may be needed. The key is to avoid as many last-minute changes as possible.

If the wedding is taking place during the summer, make sure that you advise the ushers that they will be expected to wear their jackets throughout the day (except for specific times that the bride and groom designate).

If the wedding is in the winter and if the weather looks stormy, the ushers may need overcoats when parking cars and whilst helping people in and out of the venue. In many cases they will be grateful for the added warmth. Before any decisions are made regarding the type or number of overcoats to purchase, talk to the groom.

Tips on Measuring for Tuxedos

When being measured for your tuxedo, you will want to make sure that the tailor measures your chest, both under the arms and over your arms when you are standing in a relaxed position. If your arms are rigid, the measurements will come back larger, resulting in a tuxedo that hangs awkwardly.

Never accept verbal measurements from any of the ushers. Measurements of the waist will need to be accurate as it is unlikely that you will be wearing a belt. Keep an eye on your ushers, making sure they give the tailor their full cooperation.

The inseam of your trousers will be measured from your crotch to the center of the shoe. If you plan to wear special shoes, high shoes, or very low shoes in the wedding, take them with you when being measured for your tuxedo so that your pants are not measured too short or too long.

When the tailor is measuring the sleeve length, they should measure from the center of your back (your backbone) over the shoulder and down to your wrist. If you prefer a little longer sleeve, this is the time to tell the tailor as sleeves are often made too short.

"*Be warm and tender, thoughtful and affectionate. A kind word gives much pleasure.*"

- John Lubbock

Chapter Two

WHERE TO STAY

As the best man you will be responsible for helping find suitable accommodation for the out-of-town ushers, relatives, and friends of the bride and groom. At minimum, you should provide them with a listing of where they could stay, keeping their budget in mind.

Other considerations include arranging transportation to the wedding ceremony, rehearsal, and other appointments and parties. Four or five weeks before the wedding, double check with any out-of-town ushers, relatives, or friends to ensure they have accommodations secured. If the wedding is large and several people are staying at one particular hotel, you might get in touch with the hotel manager to see if you can block off several rooms for a discounted rate. This is common practice and a great way to save money.

If you should discover that a particular family or usher is on a limited budget, arrange for them to stay with you or another one of the ushers. This can be done in a diplomatic manner to avoid embarrassment and will be appreciated.

Transportation

If people will be flying in for the wedding, be sure to arrange for transportation from the airport to wherever they will be staying. Ask the individual if they prefer a rental car or having someone pick them up.

Regarding transportation, it would be a good idea to talk to the groom at least four weeks before the wedding about the types of vehicles he would like after the ceremony. Typically, limousines are rented for this special occasion, and he may ask that you take care of the arrangements. Similar cars, trucks, or mid-sized luxury cars are used to transport the wedding party from the ceremony to the picture location and then to the reception hall.

Determine if you or the groom will be taking care of this responsibility, and if you are expected to arrange the transportation, be sure to have enough cars to accommodate the number of people in the wedding party.

Additionally, do not overlook any children who are involved in the wedding as they may need transportation as well.

If you want to save a little money, consider similar type of cars that relatives or friends of the bride or groom already drive and see if they would be willing to provide some of the transportation. Although the maid of honor and bridesmaids' dresses will take up some room, just be sure that the car leaves enough room for the bride and her dress, which, depending on her choice, could be substantial.

Boutonnieres

The bride will be responsible for picking out the flowers and the boutonnières that she wants the groom, best man, and ushers to wear. However, as the best man, you should know all the details of the florist, where the flowers are being delivered to, the time of delivery, and who to call if they do not arrive on time. Once the flowers have been delivered, ensure that everyone is wearing the appropriate boutonnière. Taking these simple, proactive steps can save a huge headache for the bride and groom.

Boutonnières add a finishing touch to the tuxedos, and even the smallest children in the wedding party should have a boutonnière to wear. Additionally, you will also be responsible for making sure that boutonnières are provided for the fathers, special uncles, and grandfathers and ensuring that they are pinned on just before the wedding ceremony.

Keep them stored in a cool, dry place until they are needed (a fridge is the ideal place).

If the bride or groom has a close loved one who is deceased, they may want to visit the grave and pay their respects. The most appropriate time to do this is after the wedding photos have been taken and when the wedding party is making its way to the reception hall.

Gloves for the Ceremony

It is becoming increasingly popular for the groom, best man, and ushers to wear gloves at more formal weddings. Again, it is your responsibility to make sure that everyone is wearing the gloves prior to the start of the ceremony and throughout.

The best man and the groom should take their gloves off just before the ceremony begins because they will both need to handle the wedding rings during the service.

At the conclusion of the wedding, it will be your duty to collect all the gloves and keep them in a safe place. The best option is to place them in a plastic bag and store them in the trunk of your car. If they have been rented with the tuxedos, they can all be returned together.

CARPET RUNNER

If the bride has rented a carpet runner, you need to have this with you when arriving for the ceremony. The ushers will then roll the carpet runner out as guests begin to arrive or before the bride walks down the aisle, whichever she prefers. After the wedding, pictures are usually taken, and this is the ideal time for you to remind the ushers to roll the runner back up and place it in whatever car you will be driving. This will ensure the carpet runner is not lost or left behind.

Car Decorations

A few weeks before the wedding, start thinking about the things that will be used to decorate the cars once the wedding ceremony is completed. As a practical joke, cans can be tied on the rear of the "getaway" car. Other options would include streamers, banners, and balloons, again tying them to the rear bumper. Depending on the type of car, window paints can be used. However, whatever you do, never use shaving cream on cars as it causes the paint to peel.

Ensure you have all the materials needed for the decorating job prior to the wedding and gather some other members of the wedding party to assist you.

In addition to the car decorations, you should also have signs already prepared that will help direct guests from the wedding to the reception.

Using white poster board and thick black markers, write the bride and groom's names on the top and then arrows pointing in the direction to drive. Be sure to place several signs coming from all the various directions. All of the guests will appreciate the assistance, and the bride and groom will be impressed!

Hanging the signs the night before the wedding would be easier; unfortunately, you risk them being stolen, damaged, or rained on. Your best option is to get up early in the morning on the day of the wedding and securely place the signs. When the wedding and reception are over, it will be your responsibility to remove them.

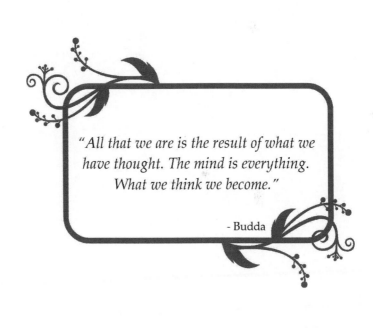

"All that we are is the result of what we have thought. The mind is everything. What we think we become."

- Budda

Chapter Three

FINANCIAL OBLIGATIONS

As the best man you will be expected to take charge, which means some financial responsibility will fall on your shoulders. The best man is expected to pay for his own tuxedo, shoes, gloves, and cuff links (if worn). The bride and groom will normally pay for all the boutonnières, other flowers, decorations, cake, music, and photographer for both the ceremony and reception.

You will also be responsible for your travel expenses if coming in from another city, which includes airfare, taxis, hotels, rental car, gratuities, and so on. Occasionally, the groom may offer assistance if you are traveling, but you should only accept his offer if you know that you cannot afford to be in the wedding otherwise.

The cost of car decorations after the ceremony as well as any other decorations that you may want to add before the bride and groom "escape" from the reception is your financial responsibility.

Expenses for the bachelor party will be your responsibility, too; this might include a van and driver, party space, special entertainment, food, and beverages. The ushers may volunteer to take up collections for the party, or the groom may offer financial assistance, but the best man should never ask.

One of the most important roles of the best man is to pay for a special gift for the bride and groom. Although your schedule is busy, this gift to the bride and groom is symbolic. Make sure you take care of this significant gesture soon after you find out about the wedding.

Bachelor Party

As the wedding nears, you should start to make the arrangements for the bachelor party. About a month before the wedding, the best man should obtain a list of relatives, friends, and ushers who should be invited to the bachelor party. If you want to make this a surprise party, you should ask the groom's parents or the bride for this list.

Several things should be remembered when planning the bachelor party. Firstly, the theme should fit the groom's style. For instance, if he is wild and likes to party, choosing a bachelor party consisting of barhopping, going to a strip club, or having a stripper to entertain is appropriate.

If the groom is more conservative, make sure that you do not go overboard with the plans and do something that will embarrass him in front of his friends and/or family.

For example, if he is shy or conservative, then you should skip the lap dance. If he is conservative but still likes to have fun, you can still barhop.

If you are planning a surprise bachelor party, you will need to make special arrangements with the bride or another close person to get the groom to the location where the party will be. For the ultimate surprise, have the bachelor party during the middle of the week when the groom will not be expecting it.

Invitations are not needed unless you are dealing with a huge number of people. Generally, the wedding party ushers, relatives, and friends will make up the invitee list. Just be sure, as the best man, that you invite all of the important people whom the groom considers his friends. After all, you want this to be a celebration involving the people who mean the most to him.

When throwing a bachelor party at a home or in a rented hall, be sure that you have a set arrival and departure time. For homes, you want to respect the homeowner's space and time, and for reception halls, you are generally paying for a set number of hours.

The food and drink are often the responsibility of the best man when the bachelor party is held in a rented hall or in someone's home. It is perfectly acceptable to ask the mother of the groom for a few goodies. Additionally, make food yourself and ask attendees to bring something with them.

Sometimes the bachelor party is held at a hotel, which is a great idea if people plan to drink. This way, you will be assured that no one will be drinking and driving. Again, if you have one particular hotel where several out-of-town guests will be staying, see if you can rent a suite or banquet room for a discounted price. Most hotels offer all the services that you want, making this option fun and safe.

The last thing you want only days before the wedding is to have someone injured by consuming too much alcohol and then getting behind the wheel of a car.

Another great idea is to hold a bonfire with kegs, either in the country or on the beach if you live near the ocean. With this option, you do not have to worry about loud music. Just be sure to check with your local city for required permits.

Having exotic entertainment is the decision of the best man. Being the best man, you should know if the groom would find this appropriate or offensive. If you decide to have a stripper entertain, make sure you work closely with the company to get exactly the type of person you want based on the groom. Strippers come in all levels of entertainment, so make sure you ask.

Regardless of the stripper, everyone attending the party needs to be advised that she is a professional and, therefore, will be treated as one.

When using an exotic dancer, stripper, or entertainer at the bachelor party, here are a few helpful tips to consider:

- ❃ Make sure you always pay with cash after the conclusion of the party.
- ❃ Point out the groom so that he will be the center of attention.
- ❃ When inquiring about fees, understand what you are paying for.
- ❃ Get everything in writing.
- ❃ Go over every expense with the business before signing on the dotted line.
- ❃ If you plan to use an exotic dancer or entertainer at the bachelor party, bring a supply of one-dollar bills with you so everyone can have a good time.

Any gifts that come from the best man to just the groom should be given during the bachelor party. Gifts for the bride and groom should be given at the rehearsal dinner, along with gifts from other guests. Once the bachelor party is over, you as the best man have the responsibility for cleanup.

If you used a rental hall, your contract may or may not include cleanup, and if the party was at a friend or relative's home, grab a few of the other men from the wedding party and have them pitch in with the cleanup.

Typically, the bride and women of the wedding party have a bachelorette party of their own, usually on the night of the bachelor party. Towards the end of the night, it is inevitable that one or the other will want to "crash" the other party. Keeping the parties separate is part of the fun and the responsibility of the best man and maid of honor.

For this reason, you and the maid of honor will need to keep in contact throughout the night to make sure nothing sneaky is going on. When parties are given together for the bride and the groom, the mood is a little different than it would be at a typical bachelor party. For shared parties, the bride and groom generally pick up all the expenses associated with food, beverages, entertainment, and invitations or announcements for location and time.

Keep in mind that shared parties are seldom done, but if the bride and groom are conservative and have family who came in from another country, this would be an excellent option.

THE WEEK OF THE WEDDING

The week before the wedding is a time of reflection and preparation to ensure that you have taken care of all the tuxedos, your clothing, and shoes and that any money owed for the ushers' tuxedos is paid. In most cases, the attire is picked up the day before the wedding.

Each person is responsible for picking up his own outfit. When you stop by to collect yours, be sure to verify that the other members of the bridal party have collected theirs as well. If any tuxedos are remaining, take them with you to save time and trouble. Additionally, ask the business owner if he or she will let the usher know you have his tuxedo with you at the church.

The decorations and details for the cars involved in the procession from the wedding to the reception should be organized and ready to attach.

Any signs for directions should be in place, and balloons and any other decorations should be up in the reception hall, which is something that can be done the night before. If any of the ushers show up looking untidy, be prepared to go to a nearby barber for a quick haircut. If no barber is available, be ready with an electric clipper and a comb.

If your wife or girlfriend will be attending the wedding with you, take a few minutes to make her feel secure about the situation. Pay compliments on her appearance, new dress, great hairstyle, and so on. She will appreciate the fact that you took the time to make sure she felt comfortable.

If you have smaller children and need a babysitter consider a responsible, mature person who can stay overnight if the reception is expected to finish late. Most receptions end on time, but if the party is still in full swing you may find it difficult to leave.

If your car will be used in the wedding procession, it would be worth the money to have it detailed so it looks and smells clean. Most of these detail services do amazing jobs, giving your car back looking like the day you bought it.

Make sure that you and everyone else involved knows the time and place of the rehearsal. It is a good idea to print out the details of the rehearsal location. You should include the address, map, date, time, and phone number of the location. Also include your cell phone number just in case anyone gets lost.

In ancient days, the best man helped the groom pack for his honeymoon, made arrangements for the pets, and literally anything else needed to make the groom's day special. In fact, the best man also cared for things that required attention while the groom was away on his honeymoon. It is your duty to remind the groom of special things that he should take on his honeymoon to please his bride.

For example, a change of clothing for leaving the reception and heading to the airport or hotel. The best man also helps the groom choose a special present for his bride as a lifetime keepsake.

As an act of friendship, the best man might even create a basket of snacks, champagne, and other goodies that the bride and groom might like to take on the honeymoon. This is especially appreciated if they will be driving to their destination.

This little care package is left in the back seat of the car that the bride and groom will use as the getaway car. Since you will be busy, the gift basket should be prepared one week in advance so it will be ready to go.

During the week before the wedding, it is good idea for the best man to remind the groom to pick up the marriage license and to put it in a safe place.

Additionally, remind the groom to prepare the envelopes needed for the caterer, the officiate, the organist or pianist, the church or hall, and any other bills that will need to be paid on the day of the wedding. Examples could be the band or DJ, the limousine service, and the florist. Each vendor will need to have his or her own envelope with the money due and acknowledgement inside.

Dealing with the Wedding Party

Because of your title—the best man—you will be expected to entertain, socialize, and organize other members of the wedding party who are unsure of what they are expected to do. If there are any members of the wedding party whom you do not particularly like, put your differences aside during the wedding, smile, and be polite.

If faced with two people in the wedding party who are fighting just for the sake of being obnoxious, it is your duty as the best man to step in, ask them to be more courteous, and remind them that this is a wedding. Nothing could be so important that they have to fight. This is a wonderful day, and everyone should have the goal of making the bride and groom happy.

"Humour is the great thing, the saving thing. The minute it crops up, all our irritations and resentments slip away, and a sunny spirit takes their place."

- Mark Twain

Chapter Four

Before Rehearsal

The rehearsal and usually the rehearsal dinner will take place the day before the wedding. The best man should contact all the ushers to ensure they have the correct information regarding time and location.

Before the rehearsal, make it clear to all the ushers that cell phones, beepers, and girlfriends will be left behind while they perform their duties. Generally, the wives and girlfriends of the ushers come to the rehearsal and usually sit together during the wedding ceremony and reception until the ushers have completed with their duties. Make sure everyone keeps all electronic gadgets in their car. As you go to the wedding rehearsal, take a moment to remind all of the ushers about the bride and groom's decision regarding body piercing.

You may hear some grumbling, but reinforce the importance of pleasing the bride and groom and honoring their request.

Follow up with the ushers to make sure they have their tuxedos and that they fit well. Ask each usher one by one if they have any last-minute details that need attending to such as shoe rental, ties, haircut, and so forth. The services of any babysitters should be arranged for the children who are not going to attend the wedding.

Before the rehearsal, any last-minute changes with cars, photos, flowers, and so forth, need to be completed. Additionally, the purchase of any liquor needed for the reception should be between the groom and the best man.

Before you make your way to the rehearsal, be sure that you take your gift for the bride and groom, a camera for fun and games, and a list of answers to any last-minute questions that need to be discussed with the groom.

Take the time to introduce people who are unfamiliar with each other as they arrive for the rehearsal. This will help to ease any tension and help to form friendships for the following day.

WEDDING REHEARSAL

Making it through the preparations to get this far is half the battle. The rest of your duties throughout the wedding will seem like a piece of cake because you are now fully prepared!

Everyone in the wedding party will need to be told where to stand, what to do at various times of the ceremony, and what will happen after the ceremony is finished. Try to remain calm and sound polite and friendly at all times whilst ensuring that the rehearsal runs smoothly

If your duties include being at the church or hall early, you will be shown where the flowers and decorations that are being delivered will be placed. During the rehearsal, artificial flowers can be used to demonstrate the correct locations for the arrangements

Although the rehearsal may seem to go slowly, take this time to make humorous remarks and have fun.

Remember that tomorrow, during the wedding, you have to remain serious and pay attention, so get all of your goofing around done at the rehearsal.

Rehearsal Dinner

After the wedding rehearsal, it is customary for the bride and groom to take the wedding party to dinner. This could be at a restaurant, in a home, or to a bar where dinner and drinks are served and last minute jitters can be talked through. This time provides the perfect opportunity for the entire wedding party to get to know one another, especially if some of them are from out of town.

At this time, the bride and groom offer gifts to those in the wedding party to say thank you for being a part of their important day. Now is the time for you as the best man to present the bride and groom with your special gift. If you would be more comfortable, you can wait until everyone has left to present your gift.

In most cases, the rehearsal dinner is not formal, but you should dress in smart clothes appropriate for the location of the ceremony.

Generally, this would mean no shorts or tank tops but a decent pair of slacks and a shirt with a collar. You are not required to wear a tie unless the dinner is formal and the bride and groom have requested it. Remember, as the best man, you hold a prestigious title and therefore need to dress to reflect this honor.

Take the time to double check with all the ushers and bridesmaids to see if they need help with anything. Sometimes the little things, such as who is riding in each car, how will they get home, where the presents should be left during the ceremony, and so on, are questions that others in the wedding party will ask. Your responsibility is to have the appropriate answers!

During the rehearsal dinner, you should address any last-minute weather changes with the groom. If the forecast is calling for rain, you will need a supply of umbrellas.

Stop by your local thrift store or dollar store and pick up several umbrellas that the ushers can use to escort people in and out of the wedding and reception.

If the day is forecast to be especially hot and sunny, the umbrellas can provide much-needed shade. It is common for the women to decorate the reception hall after the rehearsal dinner. If the men plan to help, make sure food and drinks are available as an enticement. Whatever you do not get finished the night before the wedding can be finished early on the morning of the ceremony. Again, as the best man, work closely with the maid of honor to see if she needs help with anything.

Before you go to the rehearsal, ensure that you have all of the decorations in place, the clothing organized, and everything else ready for the big day. The rehearsal and rehearsal dinner will take up most of your evening.

If the wedding party stays out past dinner or goes to decorate the hall, you might find yourself getting home in the wee hours of the morning, cutting into your sleep.

GIFT GIVING TIPS

The best man gives so much to the bride and the groom throughout the wedding, yet it is still proper and expected for the best man to give a gift as well. The perfect gift is easy to find, and you do not have to spend a fortune.

If the bride and groom have registered at any of the local retail stores, the wedding guests will have a specific place to shop, knowing exactly the items the bride and groom would like for their new home. It does not mean that you have to buy the most expensive thing on the list, but you will get some great ideas as to the types of things they want and need.

Remember that you can always go to other stores, buy it online, or find it for sale where you can save a few dollars. If the bride and groom are not registered in any of the local stores, use what you know about them to choose the perfect gift.

If the couple has lived together before getting married, buying can be difficult since it is likely they will have everything they need. In this case, choose gifts that will enhance or embellish their existing tastes such as:

- A picture frame
- Matching robes
- Towels
- Creative mixture of photos of the couple that they can hang in their home
- Gift certificates
- Matching bedroom lamps
- Memory book to be filled in over the years
- Six month supply of movie tickets so they can still date

The gift that you choose should reflect something that you know about their love for each other, their interests in the world, and something that they will find useful.

If you are stuck for ideas, a card with the gift of money is always appreciated and something every couple can use.

"Love is a choice you make from moment to moment."

- Barbara De Angelis

Chapter Five

NIGHT BEFORE TRADITIONS

The best man does have one obligation the night before the wedding—to keep the groom from being with the bride. It is tradition that the groom does not get to see the bride on the day they are married until they are at the wedding ceremony. Therefore, the best man should take the groom somewhere overnight where the bride will not be.

If the couple is living together, often the groom will stay with the best man or with his parents. If the groom needs anything from the house, the best man or one of the ushers should pick it up for him on the way to the ceremony.

When the groom has his own apartment or home, the best man should escort him to ensure he stays there and does not need anything else that night.

The groom and best man determine the time for them to meet in the morning to dress and get ready for the wedding.

Best Man Night Before Fun

The night before the wedding is often when the best man gets to have a little fun. For example, he may kidnap the groom or sometimes the bride and leave the other stranded, fending for themselves for a few hours. The decision whether to kidnap the bride or the groom belongs to the best man.

Generally, they will go to a bar and have a few shots for the upcoming celebration. Many brides and grooms have stumbled out of bed the morning of the wedding to find that they have quite a hangover. Remember that all of this is done in fun and should not be taken too seriously.

The best man will often employ the use of the ushers the night before the wedding to torment the groom in the middle of the night. They may stand outside of the groom's house or wherever he is staying and play loud music, taunting the groom to "come out and play."

In general, they will do anything they can to prevent the groom from getting a good night's sleep. Sometimes the best man will steal the keys or the car itself so the groom will be aggravated the next morning, wondering where he left his car.

Other times, the best man and the ushers will steal all the phones from where the groom is staying so there is no way for him to contact his bride the night before the wedding.

It is the best man's responsibility to make the night as memorable and fun as possible. Therefore, use your sense of humor and make sure the groom has a night that he will never forget, but without hurting him or causing him to be late for the wedding!

Hours before the Wedding

As the best man, you will be a busy person before the wedding actually takes place. Be prepared to offer assistance at the groom's house as he gets ready for the wedding. All of your hard work and planning up to this point will be paying off as you help get the groom to the ceremony and get on with your other duties.

Arriving at the groom's house, the best man will usually have a bottle of champagne for a small celebration before the ceremony. Keep in mind that this is not to say that you should be getting the groom drunk, but just helping to keep him calm.

As the best man you should help the groom to dress, run to the store for any last-minute items, and undoubtedly you will be fielding questions or calls from the ushers about where they need to be and the time to be there. Your cell phone will come in handy at times like this.

When the ushers arrive, make sure that everyone has their ties, belts, and shoestrings and that their tuxedos are in proper order. Then you will start passing out the boutonnières and anyone who needs help in pinning them on. This is also a good time to have a camera handy so you can capture any great moments to give to the couple after they are married.

Remind the groom that he needs to have everything packed and in the car, ready to leave after the reception. If the bride and groom will not be leaving immediately after the reception, the groom's house will need to be put in some type of order so when he brings his bride home things will be clean and tidy.

If the bride and groom will be staying at a hotel for the night, their bags should be placed in the car so they are ready for them. If their accommodation is nearby, one of the ushers can deliver the luggage to the hotel for storage until the bride and groom arrive later in the evening.

Make sure you get the bride's wedding ring from the groom at this time, putting it inside your coat pocket for safekeeping until the ceremony. As the best man, you will also have the marriage license and any envelopes that need to be passed out during the event, and remember to take a comb for the photos!

At one time, the ring bearer did bring the ring to the front of the ceremony on a pillow. This tradition has now been replaced where the ring bearer will carry fake rings to the front of the church, carefully tied onto a silk pillow.

You might also consider taking a small bottle of cologne with you for the ushers as some of them will be younger and will not yet have learned the value of smelling good. You want them to look and smell good for the grand occasion.

If anyone has a problem with his shoes being too slippery, put a piece of tape on the bottom with the sticky part on the outside.

This will help build up a bit of traction, ensuring there are no accidents.

Another option would be to take a piece of sandpaper and rub it over the bottom of the shoes to create traction without being noticeable.

If the weather is not cooperating by giving you a sunny day, be sure to carry a rag with you to the ceremony so that all of the ushers and the groom can quickly polish their shoes before the ceremony.

To the Wedding

The best man will take the groom to the location of the ceremony at least thirty minutes before the wedding is scheduled to start. Often the best man and the groom will arrive in the car that will take the bride and groom from the ceremony to the reception. If a limousine will be used, you would drive another car that will later be used to take the remainder of the wedding party to the reception.

Arriving at the ceremony, you should escort the groom to the appropriate waiting area, making sure he has no opportunity of seeing his bride before the wedding. If needed, have one of the ushers tell the groom where the bride is located so he knows the areas to avoid.

Once at the wedding, you will pass out the remaining boutonnières and greet elder family members as they visit with the groom before the wedding.

Pictures are always being taken before and during the wedding, so keeping a smile on everyone's face is important.

If you and the groom have to wear overcoats or hats or use umbrellas because of the weather, have the ushers put these in the car so they can be used when going into the reception. After the ceremony, little time is available to put these items back on, and if not stored in the car they could easily be forgotten.

You can check in on the bride and her party to ensure that they have everything that they need. Whilst walking around, deliver all of the envelopes to their respective recipients such as the organist, the officiate, and all the other vendors.

When handing over the envelopes, tell each individual that these are being presented by bride (name) and groom (name) with a sincere thank you.

When talking with the ushers, explain that they should be escorting guests using their right arm, walking from the back of the church to the front. Your role as the best man also means that you will need to instruct the ushers to give special care to any disabled, elderly, or special guests whom the bride or groom has invited and to ensure they are taken to the reserved special seating.

Additionally, as the best man, you will arrange when the carpet runner will be placed down the center aisle, arrange the person responsible for laying it down, and arrange the person responsible for taking care of it once the ceremony is over. Rented carpet runners are expensive if not returned on time.

For this reason, you need to instruct that the carpet runner be placed in the trunk of the waiting car that you will be traveling in to ensure it is returned on time and not forgotten. Before the ceremony begins, be sure to instruct the responsible party for decorating the cars.

You will also be responsible for knowing where the materials are, what cars need to be decorated, as well as following any other special instructions that the groom might have given to you.

If needed, friends of the family, extra ushers, or brothers and sisters of the bride and groom who are not in the wedding can do the decorating.

During the Wedding Ceremony

With the wedding almost ready to start and all the guests seated, the mother of the bride and the parents of the groom are seated. The role of the best man is to stay with the groom, calming him and making sure that he is ready to proceed.

You will also organize the procession, arranging the couples according to how the bride and groom have designated, and then you and the groom take your places at the front of the church, waiting for the wedding party and the bride to start their procession.

Before the bride walks down the aisle, double check that the ring is still in your pocket and talk to the groom, keeping him calm. Remember that these are your main duties and, as the ceremony continues, remind the groom as to where he should be standing and, if needed, what he needs to do next.

Keep in mind that everything that happens during the ceremony has already been practiced during rehearsal. Additionally, the officiate performing the ceremony takes on the responsibility of ensuring nothing goes wrong by guiding the best man and groom as necessary.

During the ceremony, depending on how nervous the groom is, you may need to offer a little coaxing when it comes time to present the ring. After the wedding ceremony is over, you as the best man and the maid of honor may serve as witnesses in signing the official documents.

After the Ceremony

When the ceremony is completed, the officiate performing the ceremony will then ask the bride and groom to face the guests and will present the couple as "Mr. and Mrs. (name)." The bride and groom will be last to leave the altar, with you escorting the maid of honor to the back of the church where wedding guests will be waiting to start the receiving line and congratulate the newly married couple.

The bride and groom will be the first in the receiving line, then the maid of honor and the best man, followed by the other members of the wedding party. You should attempt to say hello to every person coming through the receiving line, even if you do not know who they are.

After the guests have left the ceremony site, pictures are taken in the church where you will be required to smile and be presented along with other members of the wedding party.

The groom usually has one picture taken with him and the best man, so this is a good time to make sure your hair is neatly combed, your boutonnière is straight, and you are standing tall and proud.

LEAVING THE CEREMONY

After pictures in the church are finished, make sure that all members of the wedding party are situated in the appropriate car. Typically, the best man and the maid of honor ride in the same vehicle as the bride and groom, with the best man driving, unless a limousine has been rented with a driver. In this case, you and the maid of honor would ride in the back with the bride and groom.

As the best man, you may need to help the groom with the bride's dress as she is settled into the car. Be sure to pay attention to the maid of honor as well, if she requires help getting into the car with her dress.

Before leaving the church, make sure you have any flowers needed for pictures that will be taken at the reception hall or for additional pictures in the cars before leaving the church.

During the ride to additional picture locations, the best man typically opens a bottle of champagne for the bride and groom to share during the drive. It is during this time that the horns are blown as the newly married couple ride through town.

The best man and the maid of honor may throw pennies or candy to people standing in the streets, which is done as a sign of good luck for the happy couple.

Pictures

When the bride and groom are ready, you and the maid of honor will go to the location where the pictures will be taken. Many times, this will be in a park, by a stream, a bridge, or somewhere romantic and special to the couple. Upon arrival you, as the best man, should help the maid of honor out of the car and the bride and groom, if needed. At this point, it is customary for the best man to step back and allow the groom to take control of what pictures should be taken.

The groom will also now be responsible for keeping the wedding party organized and in good spirits. After all your hard work earlier, your duties are now limited, and all you have to worry about is smiling and having a good time. It is important to remember that the pictures will be taken at different times.

Just remember that you never know when the photographer will take pictures, so try to keep a nice smile on your face and show that you are enjoying the day. Staying focused on what is going on and helping to arrange the smaller children when needed are things that are important to the bride and groom, and they will appreciate your help.

When the actual wedding pictures are being taken, it is not a time to be joking and goofing off since the pictures are expensive and the photographers' time is valuable. Take responsibility for being prepared; the bride and groom would be disappointed if you were not properly buttoned, smiling, and attentive when it is time for pictures to be taken.

Do not forget that these pictures will provide a lifetime of memories for the bride and groom; therefore, you should do everything possible to make them exceptional.

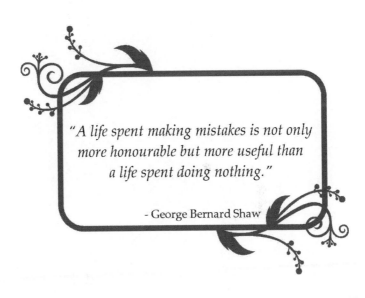

"A life spent making mistakes is not only more honourable but more useful than a life spent doing nothing."

- George Bernard Shaw

Chapter Six

TO THE RECEPTION

After the pictures are completed you, as the best man, you should help the maid of honor back into the car and offer help for the bride and groom if it is needed. Generally, if the best man is driving, he will lead the way for the entire wedding party to follow in the other cars. However, other times the car driven by the best man will be the last in the procession, making sure everyone arrives safely.

When arriving at the reception, you should park the car as close to the entrance as possible, allowing the bride and groom to enter the reception quickly. Once they are inside, make sure the remaining members of the wedding party are in order for entering the reception hall. At this point, all of the wedding party except for the bride and groom can make their way to the wedding table.

Once the rest of the wedding party is seated, an announcement is made introducing the newly married couple, who at that time enter the reception to cheers.

Reception Obligations

When the wedding ceremony is over, you will feel so relieved that your duties are almost done...although you're not finished yet! Before the end of the day, you will have a few more things to assist with in regards to pictures and the reception.

You are expected to escort the maid of honor and the bride and groom to the reception from the ceremony. Between the wedding ceremony and the reception location, you will more than likely be required to pose for pictures with the new couple, the maid of honor, family, friends, and distant relatives so remember to keep on smiling!

Remember that not only will your bright smile be seen in pictures, but also on the video. For this reason remember to smile during the wedding as the maid of honor enters the church, when you walk into the reception, and all throughout dinner.

The entire wedding party will walk into the reception hall two by two, with the newly married couple waiting to enter last so they can be introduced. Leading the maid of honor to her seat, you should pull out her chair and then gently push it in just a little as she is seated.

If the wine, champagne, or other beverages are on the table, you should pour a glass for everyone in the wedding party. Instructions from the bride should come before the wedding on who is too young for alcohol, as well as any special needs for the drinks.

You should also walk to the table where the bride and groom's parents are seated to pour a glass for them as well, which will be used to toast the bride and groom. This should be done regardless if the reception is catered or not. Sometimes the bride will prefer that the pouring of the drinks be your responsibility, while other times, the bride may prefer another person take care of this task.

Be sure to ask the bride a few days before the wedding how she would like this handled. Additionally, determine if any special guests will need your help in pouring the drinks.

After the drinks are poured and the bride and groom have made their way to the table, this is the point when some of your obligations as the best man become relaxed.

Many times, the best man will tap his spoon lightly on his glass or on his plate as encouragement for the bride and groom to kiss for the guests. Typically, the guests will chime in until the bride and groom finally give in and display their love for each other.

"Life is a promise; fulfill it."

- Mother Teresa

Chapter Seven

BEFORE DINNER

After the guests have all been seated, the toasts and speeches will start. The best man, the father of the bride, and often the father of the groom will speak special words. Other individuals may be added to this list for offering the bride and groom a toast, or if preferred, the list can be kept short, all depending on the bride and groom's preference.

Traditionally, you as the best man will offer the first toast and speech of the evening, which generally includes something special about the couple. You will offer best wishes, love, and happiness among other things. The toast itself is usually limited to a few brief comments to ensure everyone has time to toast and the reception can get started.

Additional toasts and comments from the groom to his bride and then from the bride to the groom are offered before or during the meal itself. If there were any special guests or relatives unable to attend the wedding, the best man would read their toast to the bride and groom while waiting for dinner to be served.

Special thanks will be given for the meal by one of the eldest members of the family, and then dinner will be served. Wedding dinners range from the very informal to highly formal, with some dinners catered and served to every guest. A popular option is to provide guests with a buffet-style meal, allowing them to serve themselves from long tables featuring a variety of food.

During dinner, as the best man, you will be seated on the side of the groom. When dinner is finished, you should deliver envelopes to the caterer, the musicians, and any other special parties at the reception hall who need to be paid.

Once at the reception, the entire wedding party can take a little breather as they relax and prepare for the wedding dances and other traditional festivities.

Once dinner is over, the bride and groom typically start making their way around the room, talking and mingling with the guests. Finally, you can relax and have fun without getting too drunk or causing embarrassment to the bride and groom.

If the groom had made any special arrangements for specific songs to be played, you will provide this list to the musicians at this time. Additionally, the photographer may be hanging around, eager to take individual pictures of guests and of the couple. Although you may be anxious to take your tuxedo jacket off, make sure you wait until the appropriate time.

After Dinner Excitement

The order of excitement and entertainment for after dinner will vary from wedding to wedding. The bride and groom will be responsible for choosing the types of activities to be included.

Typically, the first dance of the evening is reserved for the bride and groom while the guests watch as the couple dance together for the first time as a married couple. During this dance, you as the best man should round up the other members of the wedding party since most likely, before the next dance, the wedding party will be introduced and expected to dance to the next song.

You have the responsibility of dancing with the maid of honor and most likely posing for pictures as well during the dance. When the wedding party has danced one song, many times the bride's father will dance with the bride.

After the bride and groom and the wedding party have finished dancing, you will be expected to continue dancing with as many of the bridesmaids as possible. The ushers should also be encouraged to dance with the bridesmaids. If the best man and the groom are brothers, it is customary for the best man to dance with his mother and then pose for pictures as well.

After the dancing, other entertainment will start. Some of the activities that follow include:

- The bride throwing her bouquet of flowers to all of the eligible females
- Removing the garter, consisting of the bride sitting in a chair and the groom removing the garter
- The throwing of the garter to all of the eligible bachelors

When the bouquet and garter have been thrown, the woman who caught the bouquet and the man who caught the garter will then take their place on the dance floor.

When they have finished dancing, some wedding receptions include the ritual of having the man place the garter on the woman's leg. Rumor has it that the higher the garter is placed, the more years of luck the new bride and groom will have. Of course, this event is completely at the discretion of the bride and groom.

One of the next activities would be the cutting of the cake. At this time, the photographer will take pictures of the bride and groom while the cake is cut, and then the bride and groom feed each other a piece of cake. Your responsibility as the best man is to encourage the cake to be smeared on the face of the person being fed. Not only is this fun, but also it makes a great picture to be laughed at for years.

Additional pictures will be taken as the cake is served to the guests at the reception. The bride and groom are now left to mingle with their guests, and you and the maid of honor should dance and encourage the guests to have a great time and to join you on the dance floor.

The Getaway Car

After the general entertainment is finished, you can now disappear to complete the decorating of the car that the bride and groom will be using after the reception.

This is often a time when the best man and the ushers have a little fun. For instance, they may cover the entire car with toilet paper so the doors cannot be opened, put bras and panties in the front seat to embarrass the bride, or fill the entire interior of the car with balloons. Many times, the best man uses creative ways to get the bride and groom noticed as they try to make a clean escape.

As the busy day ends, the best man usually ensures the luggage is in the getaway car and that items such as airline tickets, hotel room keys, or special requests from the groom are taken care of before leaving.

This would be the perfect time to place a special basket of champagne or wine with cheese and crackers in the car for the bride and groom to enjoy on their first night as a couple.

As the best man, your duties are close to being completed for the night, but before the night ends, return to the reception and have a great time.

During the Reception

If the groom has forgotten to take care of anything like shutting the windows in the house or stopping the mail, make sure you take time to chat with the groom when he is free to see what you can do to help.

When the bride and groom are mingling with their guests, dancing, and having a good time, you along with the ushers should keep track of the bride to ensure the groom cannot get to her to take her away on the honeymoon. This will lead to a big dance taking place and the groom fighting his way through the crowd to get to his wife. When the groom reaches the bride, he will take her away from you and leave in the car.

Typically, the best man and the maid of honor walk out with the bride and groom to wish them luck and happiness.

"If you didn't start the day with
a smile, it's not too late to start
practising for tomorrow."

- Anonymous

Chapter Eight

AFTER THE WEDDING

After all the festivities are complete, you will feel a sense of gratification for all the hard work. This experience is an honor and something you will cherish for the rest of your life.

Now that the couple is on their way to the honeymoon and the guests have all gone, just a few things need to be completed.

The reception hall will need to be cleaned up, rented tuxedos returned, any other items rented returned, the church cleaned, food stored or given to a shelter, and finally, the gifts taken to their waiting place until the happy couple returns home.

As you can see, your responsibility of being the best man is an important one and an honor not to be taken lightly. The duties you perform will play a huge role in the success or failure of the wedding.

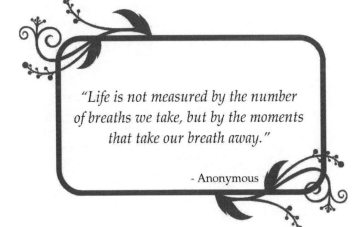

"Life is not measured by the number of breaths we take, but by the moments that take our breath away."

- Anonymous

Chapter Nine

SAMPLE TOASTS

Sample 1

When _____ first asked me to be his best man, I was truly thrilled and honored. (You may consider adding a clause or two here about the nature of your relationship with the groom.)

I still am honored.

Though, I have to admit, after the initial thrill wore off, the realization hit me that at some point I would have to get up and give a speech, which was definitely less thrilling.

I really wracked my brain as to what to say. Be funny, I thought. Well, that's easier said than done. Heck, _____ proves that every day. Believe it or not, (s)he actually thinks (s)he's funny!

(You could mention the bride, the groom, or even a relative or the bride or groom himself, if it is appropriate.)

Then I thought, just give them really good advice. Now that was something I could do:

Remember, always wear clean underwear. If you have none left…well, why don't you do some laundry once in awhile!

Remember, look both ways before crossing the street. Of course, just which two ways they are referring to, I am not sure but it still sounds good.

Remember, don't ever give me a drink before giving a toast, ever again!

So perhaps, the advice thing didn't work out so well after all.

That's OK; I have other ideas. I was told, "Say some nice things about the bride and groom."

Hmmm.
Ummm…
Hmmm…
Ummm…

Well, OK, let me get back to you on that one. I guess by now _____ is rethinking his selection in a best man, but luckily for me, it is really too late for him to do anything about it.

Oh, there you go, I just thought of something nice to say about _____… He was smart enough to pick me as his best man. (You may consider adding a quick story here if there is an appropriate one about your adventures together.)

But, getting back to the toast, I thought perhaps the best thing to do would be to find some amazing quote, some beautiful sentiment, and blow everyone away with it.

I spent quite a bit of time finding one and truly found the perfect one.

But then, after watching the ceremony, I realized the most beautiful sentiment of all was seeing _____ and _____ looking into each other's eyes.

I watched as two wonderful people pledged their love and their lives to each other, in front of their family and friends...and that blew me away.

I think we all were fortunate today as we were witness to a truly special moment. I ask that everyone please stand and raise your glasses. _____ and _____.

Thank you for allowing me to be a part of this very special day. Thank you for allowing all of us to share in your love. May God bless you both, may your love for each other continue to grow, and may today be the first day of the rest of your lives, which should be filled with health, happiness, and love.

_____ and _____, here's to you!

Sample 2

I would like to start out by acknowledging a very special lesson my grandmother taught me—a rule to live by, above all other rules. She said to me, "If you have nothing nice to say, say nothing." (Start to walk away as if you are done.)

OK, just kidding.

My grandmother actually used to say, "If you have nothing nice to say, sit next to me."

Strange how everyone wanted to sit next to her. Speaking of strange. Who picked out these bridesmaid dresses? I mean, clearly today is about _____. And she didn't want anyone else to get a smidgen of the spotlight, and I must say, in those dresses, she accomplished just that!

Its almost like that TV show *What Not to Wear*, or *Bridesmaids Gone Wild*. Come on now, _____, I am only kidding. They aren't really awful.

OK, OK, they really are but that's not what we are here for tonight. Tonight we are all here to celebrate the marriage of _____ and _____, two people who were clearly destined to be together.

Destined to be together—doesn't that just sound good? It was DESTINY. They were DESTINED.

Doesn't it really just mean that no one else would want either of them, so they had no choice but to get married? I mean really, when you boil it right down to the bare facts, I'm pretty sure that's the case here.

But whatever the reason these two got together and got married, whether it be…destiny… chance…fate…a bottle of wine and no better prospects…a blank check from _____'s father. Whatever the reason, it doesn't matter. (Be sensitive here; judge which of the above items you include based on the history of the bride, the groom, and/or their family members.)

What matters is we are all here tonight for one very special reason. To give gifts! So please, eat quickly, don't rack up a big bar tab, drop off your gifts on your way out, and drive safely.

In case of a sudden drop in pressure, airbags will drop from the overhead in front of you. (During this portion do the hand motions that a flight attendant would do on a flight.)

If we need to evacuate for any reason, there are aisle safety lights, or just follow the screaming flight attendant.

Now that you have been given that advice, let me share with you the advice I was given on how to give this toast.

I was told things like: "Hey, just picture everyone in their underwear." And I got to tell you something. Some of you people should really rethink your underwear selections.

I mean a red lace thong, really, Mr. _____, in the future please wear underwear with MUCH more material. (You may either mention the groom's father, or the bride's father, or select someone else to look at and fill in the blank.)

I was told, "Don't say anything embarrassing to the bride or groom." Well, if that's the case, they shouldn't have opened the bar before handing me the microphone! Alcohol + me + microphone = a recipe for disaster!

Another wise person said, "Remember: KISS."

Heck, I thought that meant I'd get a chance to make out with the maid of honor, then, much to my dismay, I was told KISS means "keep it short, stupid." Hey, I got the stupid part down, and one out of three ain't bad!

I have to say, the best advice I got was still my grandma's. And if you ain't got nothing nice to say, say nothing at all. So keeping it short, proving I'm stupid.

Let's all just raise our glasses and give a toast to
_____ and _____.

May your lives be full of happiness.
May your fridge be full of beer.
May your days be touched with sweetness.
And may your love grow throughout the years!

_____ and _____,
                                    here's to you!

Tonight it is my true honor to be able to toast such a wonderful couple. It is so rare in this day and age to see such love and to truly know that it is a love that will last for a lifetime.

In a world that oftentimes seems out of control, where people sometimes seem to forget about patience and kindness, it is refreshing to see pure love.

When I see a love like _____ and _____ share, it reminds me of how much beauty can come, no matter the surroundings. (You may consider adding a quick story here if there is an appropriate one.)

A day like today reminds me of a saying. I believe Confucious said: "I am reminded of the lotus flower that grows from the mud. I am reminded of the butterfly that transforms from a caterpillar. I am reminded that Botox is truly a gift from God."

Tonight we are celebrating much more than the coming together of two lives. We are also celebrating the coming together of two families.

There are certainly going to be many ups and downs in the road ahead of you. But remember, if not for the downs, you would never be able to appreciate the ups.

There will certainly be many laughs and many tears. But if not for the tears, the laughs would seem less special. There will be many losses and many victories. Remember to mourn the losses but also to celebrate the victories.

Remember how you feel tonight as there will surely be days you wonder what you were thinking. Most of all, remember that every single person in this room loves you both and wishes you nothing but happiness and love.

So please join me in raising your glasses to _____ and _____.

To the happy couple, who share a love that most could only envy, few could ever match, and none could ever surpass.

_____ and _____, here's to you.

It is customary to start a toast with welcoming the family and friends of the bride and groom to the reception.

But tonight, I wanted to part from tradition and instead toast the truth. So, rather than thank you each for coming, on behalf of the bride and groom, I will just say, "Thank you for your gifts." For after all, isn't that the real reason we have all been invited here? To give a gift.

Oh sure, the happy couple will try to claim that they wanted us to help them celebrate their union.

Oh please, who are they kidding?

Their celebration doesn't happen until they get to the hotel room, and I don't think we'll be getting an invite there...will we?

The morning after talk would be much more interesting.

Weddings like that would actually help make men want to go to them rather than spend the entire car ride to the wedding getting a list of dos and don'ts from the ladies.

Oh, now guys, you know what I mean. You know you were given your warnings. Let's see a show of hands from the guys in the room.

How many of you here got "warnings" from your wife, girlfriend, mother, whomever, before you arrived?

Come on, be honest.

Those of you with your hands raised, I congratulate you on being bold enough to admit it, being man enough to raise your hand with no fear of the ramifications later. Oh, and believe me…there WILL be ramifications.

To you liars with your hands still down…I congratulate you because, unlike the schmucks with their hands in the air, you may actually get a little loving tonight!

Now for those of you wondering if I plan to say anything about the bride and groom tonight— get over it! The check from _____ didn't clear yet! If you give me an open bar and a microphone, hey, you are asking for trouble! I cannot be held responsible.

But I would seriously like to say that it is an honor being here this evening as _____ and _____ celebrate their love for each other.

At the ceremony, as I watched these two beautiful people join their lives together, I was surprised how much it touched me, sitting and watching _____ say "I do." And it wasn't even preceded by "HEY, anyone want another beer?"!

The groom and I go way back. I cannot imagine what my life would have been like if they were not in it. We have been through so much; we know each other's hopes and dreams, our accomplishments and failures, and our proudest moments and darkest secrets.

By the way, for $29.95 you can download some video of _____ off the internet from WWW – IM A BIG MESS DOT COM.

Seriously though, I would like to congratulate _____ and _____ on their wedding day. Today truly is the first day of the rest of your lives.

Tonight is a magical night for you both, one that you are sure to look back on for a long time...and wonder why you asked me, of all people, to give a toast.

Now friends, family, invited guests, party crashers, people wondering what the heck you are doing here, please raise to your feet and lift your glasses. For those of you not wearing antiperspirant—you know who you are and so do we—please only lift your glasses shoulder height.

Let's lift our glasses and wish _____ and _____ many years of happiness, health, and love.

May God bless you and watch over you, may the rest of your lives be as special as tonight, and may you remember this toast as it is unlikely I will ever be asked to give another one.

_____ and _____,

here's to you!

QUOTES WORTH QUOTING

People need loving the most when they deserve it the least.

—JOHN HARRIGAN

Patience with others is love, patience with self is hope, patience with God is faith.

—ADEL BESTAVROS

One word frees us of all the weight and pain of life: that word is love.

—SOPHOCLES

Now join your hands and with your hands your heart.

—WILLIAM SHAKESPEARE

Love one another and you will be happy. It's as simple and as difficult as that.

—MICHAEL LEUNIG

Love is the triumph of imagination over intelligence.

—HENRY LOUIS MENCKEN

Love is stronger than justice.

—STING

Love is an emotion experienced by the many and enjoyed by the few.

—GEORGE JEAN NATHAN

Love does not consist in gazing at each other, but in looking outward together in the same direction.

—ANTOINE DE SAINT-EXUPERY

Love cures people, both the ones who give it and the ones who receive it.

—DR. KARL MENNINGER

Life is to be fortified by many friendships. To love and to be loved is the greatest happiness of existence.

—SYDNEY SMITH

Life is the flower for which love is the honey.

—VICTOR HUGO

In the arithmetic of love, one plus one equals everything and two minus one equals nothing.

—MIGNON MCLAUGHLIN

A friend is one who knows us, but loves us anyway.

—FR. JEROME CUMMINGS

Everybody can be great...because anybody can serve. You don't have to have a college degree to serve. You don't have to make your subject and verb agree to serve. You only need a heart full of grace. A soul generated by love.

—MARTIN LUTHER KING, JR.

He to whom this emotion is a stranger, who can no longer pause to wonder and stand rapt in awe, is as good as dead: his eyes are closed.

—ALBERT EINSTEIN

Hatred paralyzes life; love releases it. Hatred confuses life; love harmonizes it. Hatred darkens life; love illumines it.

—MARTIN LUTHER KING, JR.

I have found the paradox that if I love until it hurts, then there is no hurt, but only more love.

—MOTHER TERESA

The love we give away is the only love we keep.

—ELBERT HUBBARD

To love someone deeply gives you strength. Being loved by someone deeply gives you courage.

—LAO-TZU

The first duty of love is to listen.

—PAUL TILLICH

The course of true love never did run smooth.

—WILLIAM SHAKESPEARE

The way to love anything is to realize that it might be lost.

—G. K. CHESTERTON

To love another person is to see the face of God.

—VICTOR HUGO

We come to love not by finding a perfect person, but by learning to see an imperfect person perfectly.

—ANONYMOUS

We cannot really love anybody with whom we never laugh.

—AGNES REPPLIER

We seek the comfort of another. Someone to share and share the life we choose. Someone to help us through the never ending attempt to understand ourselves. And in the end, someone to comfort us along the way.

—MARLIN FINCH LUPUS

In dreams and in love there are no impossibilities.

—JANOS ARANY

Love is a choice you make from moment to moment.

—BARBARA DE ANGELIS

With love and patience, nothing is impossible.

—DAISAKU IDEDA

To be capable of steady friendship or lasting love, are the two greatest proofs, not only of goodness of heart, but of strength of mind.

—PAUL AUBUCHON

This is the miracle that happens every time to those who really love; the more they give, the more they possess.

—RAINER MARIA RILKE

Grow old along with me, the best is yet to be.

—ROBERT BROWNING

I love you not only for what you are, but for what I am when I am with you.

—ELIZABETH BARRETT BROWNING

Marriages are made in heaven and consummated on Earth.

—JOHN LYLY

QUINTESSENTIAL WEDDING GUIDES ...
AVAILABLE FROM

blue ink des/gns

WWW.BLUEINKDESIGNS.COM